INDIANS OF THE NORTHEAST

TRADITIONS, HISTORY, LEGENDS, AND LIFE

THE NATIVE AMERICANS

INDIANS OF THE NORTHEAST

TRADITIONS, HISTORY, LEGENDS, AND LIFE

LISA SITA

Gareth Stevens Publishing

A WORLD ALMANAC EDUCATION GROUP COMPANY

Please visit our web site at: **www.garethstevens.com**
For a free color catalog describing Gareth Stevens'
list of high-quality books and multimedia programs,
call 1-800-542-2595 (USA) or 1-800-461-9120 (Canada).
Gareth Stevens Publishing's Fax: (414) 332-3567.

Library of Congress Cataloging-in-Publication Data

Sita, Lisa, 1962-
Indians of the Northeast: traditions, history, legends, and life / by Lisa Sita.
p. cm. — (The Native Americans)
Originally published: Philadelphia, PA: Courage Books, © 1997.
Includes bibliographical references and index.
Summary: Describes the daily lives, culture, beliefs, social structure, and
environment of some of the diverse Native American peoples who lived in the
northeastern part of North America when the Europeans began to arrive.
ISBN 0-8368-2646-9 (lib. bdg.)
1. Indians of North America—Northeastern States—Juvenile literature.
2. Woodland Indians—Juvenile literature. [1. Indians of North America—Northeastern States.
2. Woodland Indians.] I. Title. II. Native Americans.
E78.E2S56   2000
974'.00497—dc21   99-058218

This edition published in 2000 by
Gareth Stevens Publishing
A World Almanac Education Group Company
330 West Olive Street, Suite 100
Milwaukee, WI 53212 USA

Original edition © 1997 by Michael Friedman Publishing Group, Inc.
First published in 1997 by Courage Books, an imprint of Running Press Book Publishers,
125 South Twenty-second Street, Philadelphia, PA 19103-4399.
This edition © 2000 by Gareth Stevens, Inc.
Additional end matter © 2000 by Gareth Stevens, Inc.

Editor: Susan Lauzau
Art Director: Lynne Yeamans
Layout: Robbi Oppermann Firestone
Photography Editors: Colleen A. Branigan and Deidra Gorgos

Printed in the United States of America

3 4 5 6 7 8 9 05 04 03 02 01

Contents

INTRODUCTION

❧

The First Americans

When we study ancient history, we often think only of Europe, Asia, and Africa. In fact, there is much to learn about the remote past of North America. Some scientists believe that at least eleven thousand years ago (and others say as many as twenty-six thousand years ago), early humans crossed a land bridge that linked Alaska with Siberia. This piece of land is now covered by the waters of the Bering Strait. But many Native Americans dispute this theory: they believe that their people originated in North America rather than traveling from Asia. Some Native American origin stories describe the first humans emerging from a world underground. Others tell of the birth of humans from the foam of waves. Some say that the first people were made by the Great Sun or from balls of mud. There are many different stories of the origin of Native Americans, but all have in common their birth in the land where they made their home: North America.

However the first Americans arrived, they thrived in the new world, spreading all across the continent. By the time Christopher Columbus arrived in 1492 the Americas were home to seventy-five million people who spoke two thousand different languages.

This book examines what life was like for the ancient Native Americans who lived in the last Ice Age and for their descendants, the various Woodland peoples who were living in the Northeast when Europeans began to settle there in the sixteenth century. As you read about the past of the Woodland peoples, you'll gain a better understanding of America's diverse cultures and rich history.

GATHERING CLUES ABOUT THE PAST

Since Native American cultures had no written language, we must rely on other kinds of records to tell us about the customs and traditions of peoples living in North America before Europeans arrived. There are three main sources that provide valuable clues about the lifeways of early peoples.

The archaeological record is one source. Archaeologists study buildings, tools, weapons, jewelry, and other objects that were made and used by ancient peoples. These items offer much information about the daily life of early Native Americans.

The oral tradition is another way of discovering important information about a culture. In the oral tradition, information is passed by word of mouth from one generation to the next. Many Native Americans today believe that some of their spiritual traditions, as well as other customs, have been passed from elders to the young for thousands of years through the oral tradition.

A third source of information is the written records of early European explorers. Many of the Europeans who first arrived in North America kept journals or wrote letters describing the way of life of the Native Americans

they met, who had not yet been influenced by European customs.

These sources together help researchers piece together a picture of life in North America before Europeans arrived.

🌿 A MAN IN TRADITIONAL CLOTHING SITS BESIDE HIS GRANDDAUGHTER, WHO WEARS A "JINGLE DRESS," A STYLE OF DRESS WORN FOR COMPETITION DANCING AT FESTIVALS CALLED "POWWOWS."

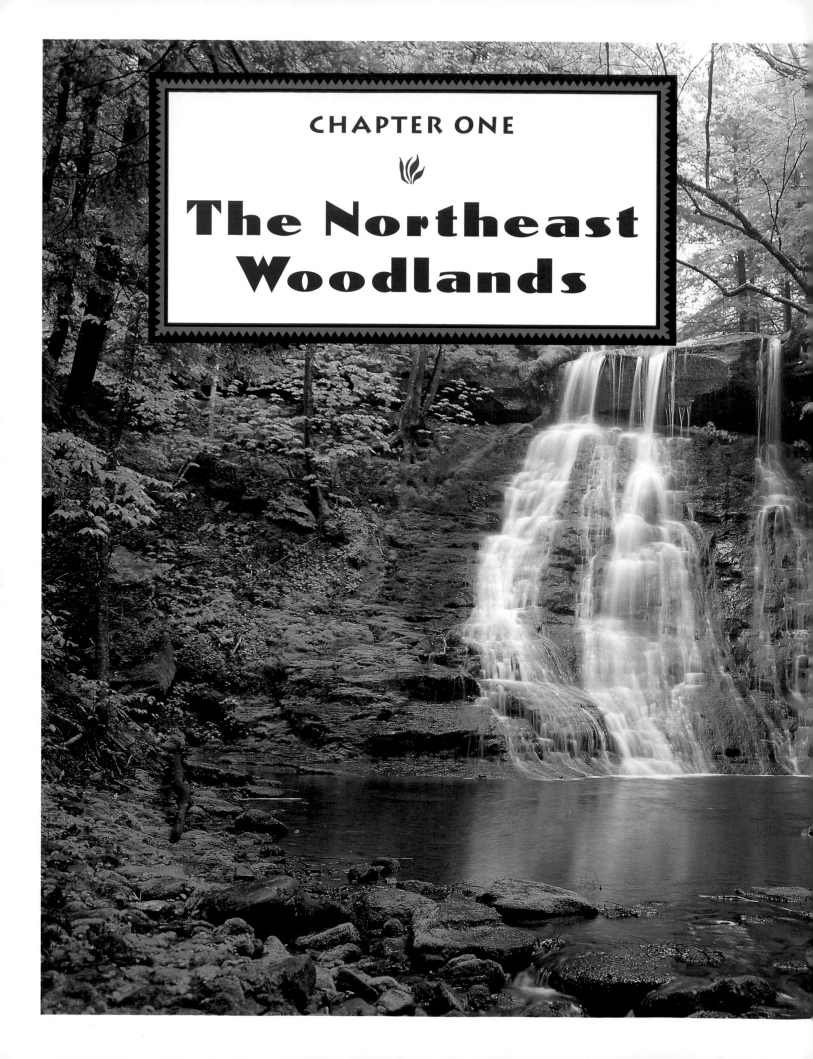

CHAPTER ONE

The Northeast Woodlands

A Land of Mountains, Lakes, and Forests

Much can be learned about particular peoples by looking at the way they adapt to and make use of their surroundings. The home of the Woodland peoples reaches up to the southern portion of Canada and extends as far south in the United States as Kentucky. East to west, the Woodland region stretches from the coast of the Atlantic Ocean to the Mississippi River. The forest continues for a short distance on the western side of the Mississippi, where it gradually gives way to the Tall Grass Plains.

 LEFT: IN THE CATSKILL MOUNTAINS OF NEW YORK, LUSH GREENERY SURROUNDS A CASCADING WATERFALL. **ABOVE:** THE SCENIC WHITE MOUNTAINS, LOCATED ON THE BORDER OF NEW HAMPSHIRE AND MAINE

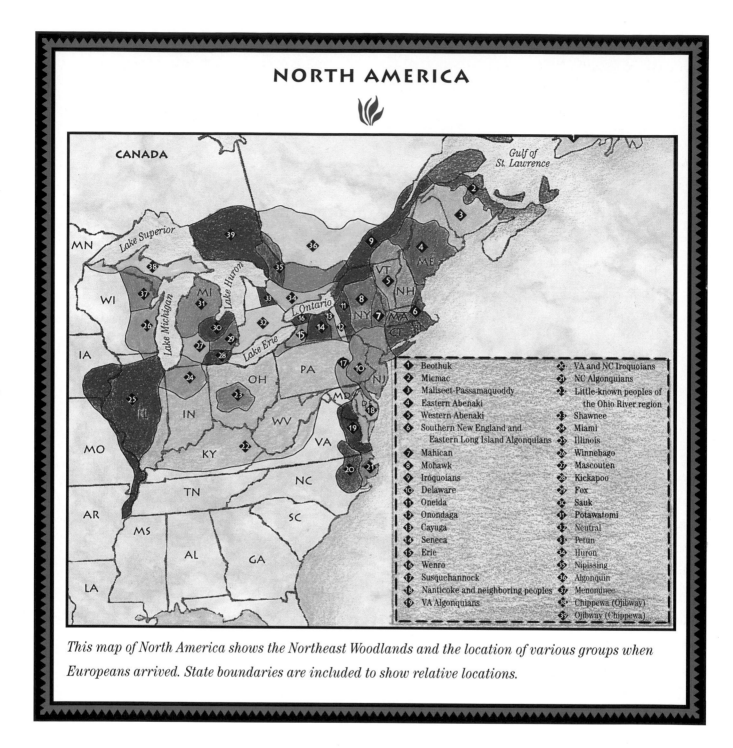

❶	Beothuk	❷⓿	VA and NC Iroquoians
❷	Micmac	㉑	NC Algonquians
❸	Maliseet-Passamaquoddy	㉒	Little-known peoples of the Ohio River region
❹	Eastern Abenaki		
❺	Western Abenaki	㉓	Shawnee
❻	Southern New England and Eastern Long Island Algonquians	㉔	Miami
		㉕	Illinois
❼	Mahican	㉖	Winnebago
❽	Mohawk	㉗	Mascouten
❾	Iroquoians	㉘	Kickapoo
❿	Delaware	㉙	Fox
⓫	Oneida	㉚	Sauk
⓬	Onondaga	㉛	Potawatomi
⓭	Cayuga	㉜	Neutral
⓮	Seneca	㉝	Petun
⓯	Erie	㉞	Huron
⓰	Wenro	㉟	Nipissing
⓱	Susquehannock	㊱	Algonquin
⓲	Nanticoke and neighboring peoples	㊲	Menominee
⓳	VA Algonquians	㊳	Chippewa (Ojibway)
		㊴	Ojibway (Chippewa)

This map of North America shows the Northeast Woodlands and the location of various groups when Europeans arrived. State boundaries are included to show relative locations.

The climate of the Northeast varies widely. Harsh, cold winters with mild summers prevail in the extreme north, while mild winters with hot, humid summers are the norm in the southern portion. Rain and thunderstorms are common from spring through autumn; cold weather brings snow or hail. Along shorelines hurricanes occasionally occur, sometimes causing flooding.

The Northeast Woodlands is a place of great natural beauty and diversity. On the coast, the waves of the Atlantic wash up on shores that, depending on their location, have either rugged, pebbly beaches or smooth shorelines of fine-grained sand. Further inland, rivers and streams run through rich, fertile valleys. Hills and mountains covered in foliage surround sparkling blue lakes.

The Northeast Woodlands abound with a wide variety of plant life. Broadleaf trees, like maple, oak, and hickory; conifers, like pine, spruce, and fir; flowering plants and trees; mushrooms and lichens; and various other forms of plant life all thrive in the forests of the Northeast. This natural garden supports a great range of animal species, including white-tailed deer, black bears, raccoons, foxes, wolves, rabbits, owls, snakes, wild turkeys, and moose.

Chippewa (or Ojibway), the Lenape (or Delaware), the Micmac, the Mohegan, and the Pequot.

Although the various groups of the Northeast had their own distinct cultures, rituals, and lifestyles, all were dependent on the Woodland environment for their natural resources. With skill and an expert knowledge of their surroundings, Woodland peoples were able to harvest the forests and waterways for all their needs. The many species of trees provided wood and bark for

🌿 A Variety of Peoples

The various cultural groups of the Northeast may be recognized as belonging to either the Iroquoian language family or the Algonquian (sometimes spelled "Algonkian") language family. It is estimated that the various groups of the Northeast Woodlands spoke at least forty different languages when Europeans first entered the region in the sixteenth century, almost all of these forty belonging to one of these two language families. (A few belonged to the Siouan language family.)

The most widely recognized of the Iroquoian peoples were the Huron (also known as Wyondot) and the Five Nations Iroquois—the Mohawk, Oneida, Onondaga, Cayuga, and Seneca. (The Tuscarora later joined the Five Nations in the early eighteenth century, making it the Six Nations.) The majority of the Northeast peoples were Algonquians, and included, among many others, the Algonquin, the

🌿 WOODLAND PEOPLE HARVESTING CORN. ORIGINALLY GATHERED AS A WILD PLANT, CORN WAS EVENTUALLY DOMESTICATED IN MEXICO, AND THE PRACTICE OF CULTIVATING IT SPREAD TO THE NORTHEAST.

WILDLIFE OF THE NORTHEAST WOODLANDS

The Northeast Woodlands teemed with animals and plants that were used by Native Americans of the area for food, clothing, shelter, medicines, and many other things. Here is a sampling of the many plants and animals found in the Northeast.

Mammals

Bear

White-tailed deer

Rabbit

Moose

Beaver

Porcupine

BELOW: EASTERN COTTONTAIL

ABOVE: PORCUPINE

Birds, Reptiles, and Other Animals

Turtle

Wild Turkey

Fish

Frog

Eagle

Bluebird

LEFT: EASTERN BLUEBIRD

LEFT: WILD TURKEY

Trees and Other Plants

Maple

Spruce

Birch

Elm

Cattail

Cherry

Chestnut

ABOVE: BLACK CHERRY TREE

ABOVE: CONE OF THE SPRUCE TREE

RIGHT:
WHITE-TAILED
DEER AND
FAWN

BELOW: BLACK BEAR
MOTHER AND CUBS

LEFT:
MOOSE

RIGHT:
PAINTED
TURTLE

LEFT:
EASTERN TREE
FROG

LEFT:
CATTAILS

LEFT:
MAPLE TREE

homes, canoes, bowls and other containers, musical instruments, and a great many other items; wild plants provided medicines, food, and raw materials for basket weaving and other crafts; animals provided meat and skins for clothing, blankets, and bags; fish and shellfish provided food and shells for crafting decorative items and wampum (a kind of money); and turtles were eaten and their shells used for musical instruments.

The peoples of the Northeast Woodlands were in tune with the changes of the seasons and understood how the changes affected the behavior of game animals and the growth of wild plants. This knowledge helped them hunt more efficiently and gather wild fruits, nuts, and vegetables at their ripest. In addition, many groups practiced agriculture. Corn was an especially important crop, and Northeast women not only cooked or baked it into foods, but made clever use of all parts of the plant, from the cob to the husk.

Embedded in the flow of everyday life were the deeply felt spiritual beliefs revealed in the rituals and ceremonies practiced by the different groups. These beliefs formed the basis of a strong and influential spiritual tradition that continues, for many Woodland peoples, into the present.

ABOVE: WHERE BIRCH TREES WERE PLENTIFUL, WOODLAND PEOPLES MADE CANOES FROM THE BARK, WHICH THEY STRIPPED FROM THE TREES IN LONG SHEETS. BIRCH-BARK CANOES WERE LIGHTWEIGHT, YET CAPABLE OF CARRYING HEAVY LOADS. OPPOSITE: IN THIS EARLY SCENE OF THE NORTHEAST, A YOUNG IROQUOIS MAN WEARS THE TRADITIONAL HAIRSTYLE OF A WARRIOR.

CHAPTER TWO

Early Life

 From the Ice Age to the Archaic

About fourteen thousand years ago, as the last glaciers in North America began to retreat, the environment of the Northeast Woodlands began to gradually change. As the glaciers melted, the Northeast became warmer. The tundra, or arctic plain, turned to grassland, which then turned to forest. The early peoples living in the region adapted to these changes.

Early Native Americans, called Paleo-Indians, living during the last Ice Age were primarily hunters of the giant mammals of the time, like the mastodon and woolly mammoth, although they supplemented their diet of meat with wild plants. But by about 7000 B.C. (nine thousand years ago) most of the large Ice Age

LEFT: ANIMALS LIKE THIS GIANT MASTODON WERE ONCE HUNTED BY THE PALEO-INDIANS. ABOVE: EARLY NATIVE AMERICANS MADE ARROWHEADS, SPEAR POINTS, AND TOOLS OF CHIPPED STONE.

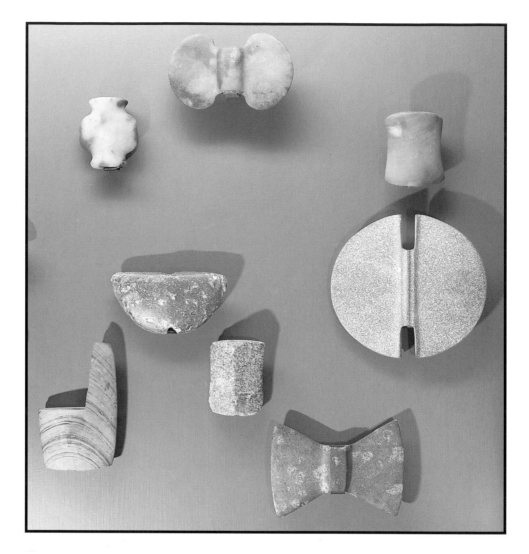

animals had become extinct in the Northeast Woodlands. No one knows exactly why these animals died out, but most scientists agree that it was a combination of changes in climate and the aggressive hunting tactics of the Paleo-Indians. The people who depended on these Ice Age animals for food and hides began to hunt smaller game like deer, elk, and bear. They also made wider use of wild plant foods and fish. This period lasted in the Eastern Woodlands from about 6000 B.C. to about 1500 B.C. and is known as the Archaic Period.

During the Archaic, early Woodland peoples lived in small groups and moved seasonally in their search for food, trading with other groups as they traveled. They ground their food with stones and probably stored some of it for use in case food became scarce. Besides grinders, peoples of the early Archaic made other types of stone tools, including knives, axes, and adzes (cutting tools used for shaping wood). As the Archaic progressed, they began to make dugout canoes from logs. They fished using spears and nets and improved their hunting weapons. In some areas, the people made circular or rectangular homes of saplings that were probably covered with bark or animal hides.

Two important cultures that developed during the Archaic period were the Red Paint People and the Old Copper Culture. The Red Paint People lived from about 2000 B.C. to about 500 B.C. in what is now New England and eastern Canada. They are called Red Paint People because of their custom of lining burial pits with red hematite, a mineral found in the region. Archaeologists believe the color red may have had sacred significance connected to their spiritual beliefs because red is the color of blood and hence life.

The Red Paint People also buried their dead with stone tools, kits of pyrite and flint used to make fire, and tools, weapons, and ornaments of bone and antler. The most well preserved of the Red Paint sites is Port au Choix in Newfoundland, Canada. Here, archaeologists have uncovered the skeletons of one hundred individuals, both male and female, about half of whom were adults, half children. Among the things found in the grave were finely made items of bone and antler, including combs, pins, and effigies (symbolic figures, usually of animals or people). Archaeologists call these items buried with the dead "grave goods."

Eventually, for reasons that are still unclear, the Red Paint People stopped practicing their rich ceremonial burials. Some archaeologists believe this is because the people moved away from the area. By 500 B.C. the ponds of the region were turning into bogs, and without a good source of water the area could no longer support large numbers of people. As many of the Red Paint People migrated out of the region, their customs and practices faded into disuse.

The Old Copper Culture developed in the western Great Lakes region about 3000 B.C. and flourished from about 2000 B.C. to about 1000 B.C. These people mined copper found in the area and skillfully hammered it into spear points, knives, sewing awls, beads, axes, pendants, and bracelets. To keep the metal from becoming brittle they practiced the technique of "annealing." This involved heating the copper and then plunging it into cold water, then repeating the process again and again. The people of the Old Copper Culture also made birch-bark containers, kept domesticated dogs, and made dugouts and possibly birch-bark canoes. Archaeologists are still unsure why the Old Copper Culture came to an end. Some think that perhaps the people of the Old Copper Culture migrated further north, away from the natural deposits of copper, while others think that the people changed their culture as the climate and environment changed.

THE KOSTER SITE

A site called Koster in present-day Illinois has yielded a great deal of information about daily life in the Northeast Woodlands during the Archaic Period. Archaeologists have uncovered well-preserved stone tools, hunting gear, and food remnants that include seeds, nuts, and bones.

At any archaeological site, as the archaeologists dig further and further into the earth, they uncover layer upon layer of dirt. Each layer is from a different time period: the deeper the layer, the earlier the time period. At Koster, archaeologists excavating these various layers have discovered many different settlements from several time periods.

Evidence at Koster shows that this site had been inhabited since at least 7000 B.C. By about 6500 B.C. the dog had been domesticated in this area. By 5000 B.C. the people at Koster were building permanent or semipermanent dwellings. By 3500 B.C. village life at Koster had become more complex, with the people building larger houses, drying fish on racks to preserve them, and roasting foods in limestone pits. By A.D. 1000 the people were farmers who grew corn as a major food source.

The Woodland Period

The Archaic gradually led to another period, called the Woodland, which began about 1000 B.C. and lasted into the period of European contact, which began in the sixteenth century. During the Woodland Period, early peoples of the Northeast developed agriculture, began making pottery, and devoted a great deal of attention to the ritual burying of the dead in domed mounds of earth.

Ritual mound burials first began in the areas of southern Michigan, Indiana, and Ohio about 1500 B.C., when people began to bury their dead in small hills made by the movement of glaciers. These natural mounds are called "kames." The people of the Glacial Kame culture buried their dead with powdered red ocher (a natural pigment), and tools and ornaments of stone, copper, and shell. By 1000 B.C., while the Glacial Kame people contin-

ued to use natural burial mounds, others in the Northeast had begun to deliberately construct mounds of earth over their dead. This new practice was the work of a culture known as Adena, named for a site in Ohio where a group of mounds was discovered.

The Adena culture developed in the Ohio Valley about 1000 B.C. and lasted until about A.D. 200. Its influence spread to surrounding areas, even as far as what is now known as Kentucky, West Virginia, New York, and Pennsylvania. The Adena people made pottery, wove textiles, and planted some crops, though they relied mainly on hunting, gathering wild plants, and fishing for their food. They lived in small communities of perhaps four or five circular homes that sheltered extended families.

The kinds of objects found in Adena burial mounds include beautifully carved and highly polished gorgets (stone disks with two holes drilled in them, used as pendants), incised tablets (probably used as stamps for applying tattoos), and smoking pipes of fine-grained stone, as well as jewelry, beads, and axes made of copper imported from the Great Lakes region.

Some of the burials were simpler than others. Simple burials contained few, if any, grave goods, and the deceased were either cremated or buried in plain, clay-lined basins over which the mounds were built. The

◖ IN THE WOODLAND PERIOD, THE PEOPLE OF THE GLACIAL KAME CULTURE MADE THIS TYPE OF OBLONG-SHAPED GORGET, KNOWN TODAY AS A SANDAL-SOLE GORGET.

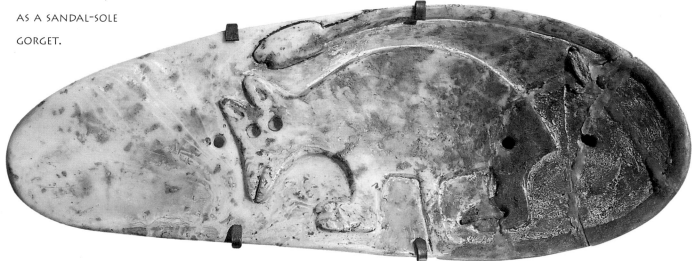

GREAT SERPENT MOUND

🌿 GREAT SERPENT MOUND, OHIO

One of the most spectacular earthworks is located near present-day Cincinnati, Ohio, and is known today as the Great Serpent Mound. As its name describes, the Great Serpent Mound is built in the shape of a colossal serpent, or snake, with an egg in its mouth. Built along a hilltop overlooking a stream, its coiled body stretches over twelve hundred feet (366m), and is thirty feet (9m) wide and five feet (1.5m) high. The outline of the serpent was made using small stones and pieces of clay as markers. Then the ancient builders piled baskets full of clay over the markers to create the giant earthwork. The purpose of Great Serpent Mound remains a mystery. Some scholars note that curves in the snake's body align with certain stars and suggest that the mound may have been built to honor or study the night skies.

While many archaeologists link the Great Serpent Mound with the Adena culture because of similar building styles, it has been difficult for scientists to date the earthwork accurately, since no artifacts have been found within it. Recently, scientists studied tiny bits of charcoal from the mound and found that they dated only from about A.D. 1070—much later than the Adena! While archaeologists search for more clues about the mound's age and puzzle over the serpent's purpose, the Great Serpent Mound serves as a giant reminder of those who came before us.

more elaborate graves were larger, and some held as many as three individuals. These graves contained more objects and the burial chambers were often lined with logs. Because of these differences in burials, some archaeologists think the more elaborate graves belonged to high-ranking persons. This kind of archaeological evidence suggests to some that the people of the Adena culture had some form of class system, with the wealthier people having fancier burials. Most archaeologists, however, think that the differences in burials are not very great and that there were no class differences in Adena society.

Besides burial mounds, the people of the Adena tradition also built large earthworks (ridges made of piled earth) in the form of circles, squares, and pentagons,

🌿 Hopewell mounds at Mound City National Historic Site, Ohio

usually with entrances leading inside the embankment. The interior spaces of these earthworks averaged 109 yards (100m) in diameter. Archaeologists think these earthworks were not made as walls for defense, but were more likely sacred enclosures used during ceremonies.

In the same region of the Adena culture, another tradition arose during the middle Woodland period. This tradition, which lasted from about 200 B.C. to about A.D. 500, is known as Hopewell (named after Mordecai Hopewell, on whose farm a large mound had been excavated in the nineteenth century). The term "Hopewell" does not refer to a particular culture. Rather, it refers to a lifestyle—including beliefs, ideas, and symbols—shared by peoples of different cultures throughout a large region.

The Hopewell tradition grew out of the Adena culture. Like the Adena peoples, the peoples of Hopewell built burial mounds and earthworks and made finely crafted grave goods. But the Hopewell peoples developed these talents to a new level. Their earthworks and mounds were more elaborate (some of their mounds contained hundreds of individuals, each buried at different times), and their burials included a greater number and wider variety of grave goods.

In creating objects for their lavish burials, the Hopewell developed a trade network that spanned North

ELABORATE RICHES

Peoples of the Hopewell tradition spared no expense in providing exquisite grave goods for the dead. The deceased were not only surrounded by an assortment of useful items, like pottery and weapons, but were artfully adorned with elaborate jewelry, breastplates, headdresses, and other ornaments. At a group of mounds known as the Turner group in Hamilton County, Ohio, a single grave contained twelve thousand pearls, thirty-five thousand pearl beads, twenty thousand shell beads, nuggets of gold, iron, and silver, beads of copper and iron, and sheets of hammered gold and copper. The Seip Mound in Ross County, Ohio, contained a twenty-eight-pound (13kg) copper ax, thousands of pearls, copper breastplates (which were worn on the chest as decoration), and an artificial nose of copper placed on the skull of the deceased.

🍂 NECKLACES AND EAR SPOOLS MADE OF COPPER AND FRESHWATER PEARL BEADS

🌿 **LEFT:** THIS PAINTING DEPICTS WHAT A HOPEWELL BURIAL CEREMONY MAY HAVE BEEN LIKE. **ABOVE:** THIS HOPEWELL POT, DECORATED IN RELIEF WITH BONES AND HUMAN HANDS, WAS USED IN A BURIAL CEREMONY.

America. Grave goods were made of materials as diverse as copper from the Great Lakes, obsidian and grizzly bear teeth from the Rocky Mountains, mica and quartz crystal from the Appalachian Mountains, and seashells, turtle shells, and shark teeth from the Gulf of Mexico and the Atlantic coastal regions.

The raw materials imported through this trade network were skillfully crafted into a wide assortment of objects: copper was hammered into beads, pendants, axes, panpipes (musical instruments), headdresses, and breastplates (decorative pieces worn over the chest); copper and mica were made into elegant cutouts of animals, geometric shapes, and human hands; iron, gold, and silver were beaten thin to make a foil that was used

MEADOWCROFT ROCKSHELTER

Archaeologists have uncovered many sites throughout the Northeast Woodlands that show evidence of humans having lived there. These sites are most often camp sites, places where early Native Americans had set up temporary shelter while traveling in search of game. Using a technique called radiocarbon dating, archaeologists are able to find out approximately when these camps were in use.

At a site called Meadowcroft Rockshelter near Pittsburgh, Pennsylvania, archaeologists have uncovered artifacts and fragments of human bone that may date as far back as 14,000 to 11,000 B.C. Evidence shows that Meadowcroft Rockshelter was used by Native Americans well into the period of contact with Europeans.

to cover objects made of plainer materials; obsidian and chert (a flintlike rock) were chipped into handsome knives and projectile points; exotic rocks and minerals were carved into tobacco pipes in animal and human form; and clay was fashioned into pottery bearing fancy designs made especially for burial.

Most excavations of Hopewell sites were carried out in the nineteenth century, when archaeology was a

SOUTHERN NEIGHBORS: THE TEMPLE MOUND BUILDERS

A few centuries after the Hopewell tradition faded, another important society grew up in the Mississippi Valley in the area between present-day Memphis, Tennessee, and St. Louis, Missouri. This tradition is known as the Mississippian. Widespread throughout the Southeast Wood-lands, its influence also reached northward into the Midwest.

The peoples of Mississippian society were farmers. They built large cities, where thousands of people gathered for public ceremonies centered around huge structures, called temple mounds. The temple mounds were earthworks shaped like flat-topped pyramids, on which were built tem-ples and dwellings for the priests and ruling class. Because of these structures, the Mississippians are also known as the Temple Mound Builders. Like the Adena and Hopewell peoples, the Mississippians built mounds in which to bury their dead. These burials included grave goods as varied and as finely crafted as those found in Hopewell burials.

🌿 A JAR WITH ANIMAL FEATURES (LEFT) AND A GORGET MADE OF CARVED SHELL (ABOVE), BOTH FROM THE MISSISSIPPIAN CULTURE

LOCATIONS OF ADENA AND HOPEWELL SITES

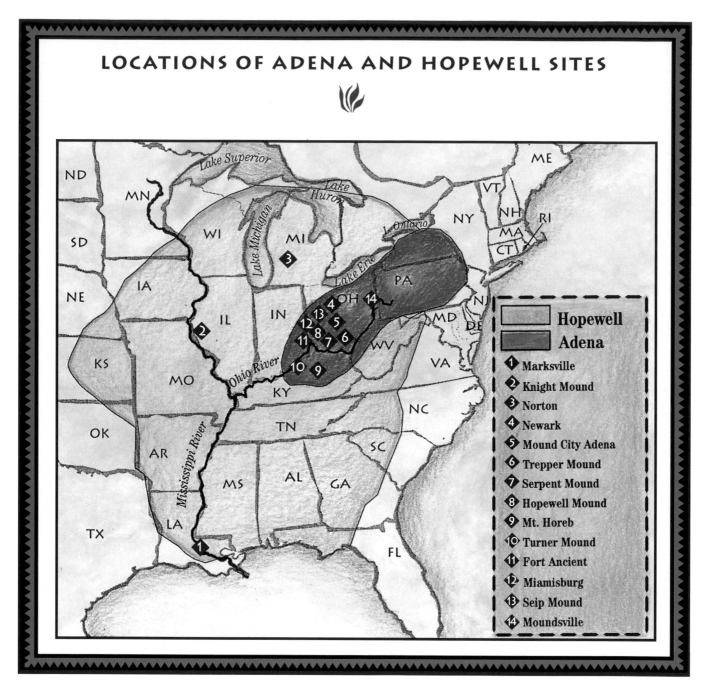

Hopewell
Adena

1. Marksville
2. Knight Mound
3. Norton
4. Newark
5. Mound City Adena
6. Trepper Mound
7. Serpent Mound
8. Hopewell Mound
9. Mt. Horeb
10. Turner Mound
11. Fort Ancient
12. Miamisburg
13. Seip Mound
14. Moundsville

young science, and amateurs carelessly destroyed the sites. As a result, little is known of the daily lives of the Hopewell peoples. What is known is that, like the Adena culture, the Hopewell practiced agriculture in addition to hunting and gathering, they lived in communities separate from their ceremonial mounds and earthworks, and they practiced weaving and pottery-making. The Hopewell created beautiful artworks, were skilled engineers, and had a highly developed ritual system focused on the afterlife. While it is not clear exactly why the Hopewell tradition faded, most archaeologists agree that the Hopewell were greatly affected by a breakdown of the trade network linking the various Hopewell peoples and supplying the materials for their exotic burials.

🌿 **OPPOSITE:** THE MOUND BUILDERS, DEPICTED HERE GATHERING THEIR CROPS. FARMING SUPPLIED FOODS TO SUPPLEMENT THEIR DIET OF MEAT AND WILD PLANTS.

CHAPTER THREE

Living off the Land

🌿 Farmers and Hunters

Throughout the Woodland period, groups of peoples in the Northeast Woodlands continued to develop lifeways that would persist well into the period of European contact. The Woodland peoples used their environment to obtain all the things they needed, from food and clothing to shelter and transportation.

All groups in the Northeast made use of the abundantly rich natural plant and animal resources surrounding them. Using bows and arrows, blowguns, snares, and pitfalls, they hunted a variety of animals,

🌿 **LEFT:** ATTRACTED BY THE TORCHLIGHT, FISH SWAM TOWARD THE WATER'S SURFACE ONLY TO BE SPEARED BY WAITING FISHERMEN. **ABOVE:** THIS BLACK-DYED DEER-SKIN POUCH EMBROIDERED WITH PORCUPINE QUILLS MAY HAVE HELD CHARMS TO ENSURE A GOOD HUNT AS WELL AS PIPES AND TOBACCO.

DEER

into soft clothing and moccasins, while the deer's sinews became the thread that held these garments together. Bones and antlers were carved into jewelry, charms, needles, and other tools.

The deer had its place in the ceremonial life of the Woodland peoples as well. Its magnificent antlers sometimes adorned the headdress of the chief, while its hooves were made into jingler rattles for use in ceremonial dances. The silvery white tail hair, too, decorated robes and headdresses worn during rituals.

Deer were very important to the Woodland cultures, and the people used the parts of the deer in many ingenious ways. The women cooked deer meat and served it fresh, or they preserved it by smoking or drying to feed their families in times when game was less plentiful. The hide was sewn

Even as the Woodland men hunted the deer, they thanked its spirit for the gifts they would receive from the animal. The food, clothing, and tools the people took from the deer helped ensure their survival in the woodlands of the Northeast.

including white-tailed deer, rabbits, and black bears. In addition to meat, most of these animals provided skins and furs for making clothing, pouches, and blankets as well as bone and antler that could be carved into utensils and tools.

The many lakes, streams, and rivers of the inland areas provided fish, which were caught using nets, traps, weirs (fences set in a stream to trap fish), and spears. One method used to attract fish when spear fishing was to go out on the lake or river at night with a lighted bark torch. The fish, drawn to the light, would swim to the surface and could be caught more easily. Along the Atlantic coast, shellfish, including crabs and clams, were gathered by the peoples living there.

The forests of the Northeast also provided a great variety of plant foods, including fruits like apples and wild strawberries, roots, mushrooms, nuts like walnuts and acorns, wild rice, maple sugar, and an assortment of

MAPLE SUGARING

Each year in early spring, groups in the northern region of the Northeast Woodlands set up maple sugaring camps deep in the woods where the maple trees grew. A gash was cut into each tree trunk and wooden spouts were inserted into the gashes. The tree sap ran down the spouts and dripped into birch-bark containers placed below them. Once collected, the sap was poured into larger containers of birch bark or wood and boiled by dropping heated rocks into the liquid. As the sap boiled and the water evaporated, the sap turned into maple syrup. Heated longer, it turned into maple sugar.

Maple sugar was used both as a food and as a seasoning. Some scholars today debate whether or not maple sugaring was done before the period of European contact. Regardless of when it originated, maple sugaring provided a favorite food enjoyed by many peoples of the Northeast Woodlands.

❦ THIS EARLY ARTIST'S DEPICTION PORTRAYS FARMING IN THE NORTHEAST WOODLANDS. THE METAL HOES USED TO TILL THE SOIL WERE OBTAINED BY NATIVE PEOPLES THROUGH TRADE WITH EUROPEANS.

plants whose leaves and shoots were cooked and eaten as vegetables. Besides providing food, many plants of the Northeast were brewed into beverages or used as seasoning or as medicine.

In addition to gathering these plant and animal foods, almost all groups in the Northeast Woodlands farmed. The exception were the groups living in the

HARVESTING WILD RICE

At the end of each summer, peoples living in the region of the upper Great Lakes went out to the swampy areas where wild rice grew. There they would harvest the rice from their canoes. Slowly steering the canoes through the waterways, surrounded by tall, grasslike stalks that held the rice, the harvesters would first tie the tops of the stalks together. A few weeks later, after the rice had fully ripened, the people returned. Once again they slowly steered the canoes while men and women

 WILD RICE, HARVESTED IN THE GREAT LAKES REGION, WAS AN IMPORTANT FOOD FOR THE PEOPLES LIVING THERE.

bent the stalks over the canoes and beat them with long sticks. This caused the rice to fall from the stalks into the canoe. Some of the rice fell back into the water, to germinate and thus ensure another rice harvest the following year. Later, the rice was dried and the hard outer covering removed.

MEDICINAL PLANTS OF
THE NORTHEAST WOODLANDS

Native Americans of the Northeast used a wide variety of plants. Roots, stems, leaves, blossoms, and, in the case of trees, bark, were used as medicines to treat sickness. Sometimes the plant was made into a poultice (a kind of moist pack made by grinding the plant) and placed over the area to be relieved, as over the head if the patient was suffering from a head-ache. Often the plant was made into a tea by boiling the roots, leaves, or blossoms and was then drunk by the patient or, in some cases, washed over the infected area. Other times plant parts were chewed and sometimes swallowed. Listed here are a few of these medicinal plants and some of the ailments they treated:

Plant	Treatment
Beebalm	Headaches, fevers, insect bites
Wintergreen	Aching joints, fevers
Bloodroot	Stomachaches, burns, sore throats, sores, ulcers
Black cherry	Coughs, diarrhea, colds, sores
Wild plum	Intestinal parasites, wounds, canker sores
Dogbane	Headaches, earaches, sore throats, heart palpitations
Elderberry	Fevers, scrapes, bruises
Goldenrod	Sores, burns, convulsions, chest pains, sprains, childbirth
Juniper	Headaches, colds, childbirth
Milkweed	Ringworm, bruises, wounds
Sumac	Skin irritations, hemorrhoids, sore throats, diarrhea
Poison ivy	Swollen glands, sores

LEFT: SEED POD OF THE MILKWEED PLANT

LEFT: POISON IVY

COOKING WITH CORN

Corn was perhaps the most important crop grown in the Northeast and was artfully prepared in a variety of ways by Woodland women. It could be roasted; made into mush, soups, dumplings, and corn pudding and ground into cornmeal for baking into bread. Combined with squash and beans, corn was also made into a stewlike dish called "succotash." Together, corn, beans, and squash provided a nutritionally balanced diet for the people of the Northeast Woodlands.

ᵂ EARS OF CORN, WITH THEIR HUSKS PULLED BACK, ARE SHOWN STILL ATTACHED TO THEIR STALKS.

ᵂ BY KEEPING WATCH OVER THE FIELDS ON SCAFFOLDS SUCH AS THESE, WOMEN, AND SOMETIMES CHILDREN, WERE ABLE TO SCARE BIRDS AWAY FROM CROPS.

northernmost regions, where crops would not grow. To clear the land for cultivation, Woodland peoples practiced slash-and-burn agriculture, in which small trees and bushes were first cut down and then burned. Crops were planted in the ashes, which provided a rich, fertilizing soil.

The most important crops were corn, beans, and squash, which were grown together in one plot. Corn was planted first. Using bone or stone hoes, these early farmers made small hills about three feet (91cm) apart; then they sowed several corn seeds in each tiny hill. When the young cornstalks had begun to grow, beans and squash seeds were added to the hills. As the plants matured, the squash grew between the hills, and the beanstalks climbed the cornstalks. In this way, the cornstalks supported the beanstalks, and the squash leaves helped to control weed growth. The Woodland peoples also grew other crops, such as sunflowers, pumpkins, and gourds.

Some groups depended on farming more than others. Although many Algonquian groups grew crops, agriculture played a more important role among the Iroquois. The Algonquians harvested most of their food from the natural environment. Many Algonquians left their villages seasonally, breaking up into smaller family units, to search for food. The Five Nations Iroquois, known simply as "the Iroquois," however, depended on agriculture for a large percentage of their diet.

Tending their crops for most of the year, the Iroquois lived in permanent villages fortified by palisades, or fences, made of tall wooden poles. They moved their villages when the nutrients in the soil were exhausted from overuse, about once every twenty years. Within the safe enclosure of the palisades, each village featured barrel-roofed, multifamily homes known as longhouses. A long-house could be as short as fifty feet (15m) or as long as two hundred feet (61m), depending on how many families lived there. (The families living in each longhouse were related through the oldest woman of the household.)

The longhouse was made by first building a frame-work of saplings and then covering this framework with large sheets of bark, usually from the elm tree. Entryways

❧ FOR PROTECTION, THE IROQUOIS PEOPLE FORTIFIED THEIR VILLAGES WITH HIGH PALISADES OF LONG WOODEN POLES.

🌿 The Iroquois longhouse was a large structure that housed several related families.

were located at each end of the longhouse and were covered with skin curtains. Inside, platforms built along the length of each wall about two feet (60cm) above the ground were divided into living areas by hanging skin curtains. Soft furs cushioned the wooden platforms for comfortable sitting and sleeping. A second platform, built above the first on each wall, served as storage shelves for food, personal possessions, and household items such as pottery, weapons, baskets, and clothing. Drying food and herbs hung from beams and rafters.

Stone-lined hearths were set into the floor along the center aisle of the longhouse. The two families whose living areas faced each other shared a single fire. Smoke

escaped the longhouse through smoke holes made in the roof above each fire. In bad weather, these smoke holes, which also let air and light into the longhouse, could be covered with bark or animal skin.

Unlike the Iroquois, the Algonquian lived in homes that usually housed only a single family or perhaps two related families. Such homes are known as "wigwams," a word derived from the Chippewa word for *home*. Wigwams were usually round, dome-shaped dwellings, although some were conical with either a circular or square base. They were made by covering a framework of saplings with bark (usually birch bark), skins, mats woven from cattail or other plants, or a combination of bark and mats. Inside each dwelling, platforms covered with skins or mats were built along the walls. Above the wigwam's central hearth was a smoke hole, which let smoke out and fresh air in. As with the Iroquois, the villages of the Algonquian peoples were often palisaded for protection.

🌿 Beautiful Bark

Northeast peoples made ingenious use of the great variety of trees the forests furnished. In addition to using wood and bark to build homes, they crafted these materials into an array of other items. Wood was cut thin and made into woodsplint baskets used for storage and carrying loads. Felled trees were made into dugout canoes by cutting them lengthwise, charring the wood with hot coals, and then digging out the wood from the center of the trunk with axes and adzes.

Canoes were also made by covering a framework of saplings with bark. Although elm bark canoes were more common because the bark was available in more

including animal and floral designs. These cutouts could then be used in one of two ways. Sometimes the cutout was placed over the surface to be decorated and outlined with a sharp tool. Then, after the stencil was removed, the bark surrounding the etched design was scraped away to reveal a lighter layer of bark underneath. The second way of using the cutout was to sew it directly onto the surface to be decorated using plant fiber as thread.

regions, birch bark made a better canoe because the end product was light (and therefore easily portable), and could carry heavy loads. Birch-bark canoes were made by peoples of the extreme northern Woodlands, where birch bark was readily available, and were often traded with groups living further south.

Woodland peoples also used bark to make rattles, torches, and various containers, including cooking pots. Birch bark, light and flexible, was the preferred material for various types of containers, including trays, dishes, buckets, storage boxes, and cooking pots. (Cooking utensils like spoons and ladles were usually made of carved wood or gourds.) Birch-bark containers were made by cutting and bending the bark into the desired shape. The sides of the container were sewn together by punching holes along the edges and lacing them together with tough plant fibers or holding them together with thin sticks.

The smooth surfaces of birch-bark containers were often decorated using bark cutouts or stencils. The artist first cut pieces of bark into various shapes,

Some birch-bark containers had lids, some had leather straps, and some had edges sealed with pine pitch. Pine pitch prevented water from leaking out of the container. A container sealed with pitch could be used to carry water or to cook soup or stew. Birch bark is a porous material. Like a sponge, the pores (tiny holes) in the bark soak up some of the liquid. The water inside the birch-bark pot kept the bottom of the pot damp and prevented the container from burning.

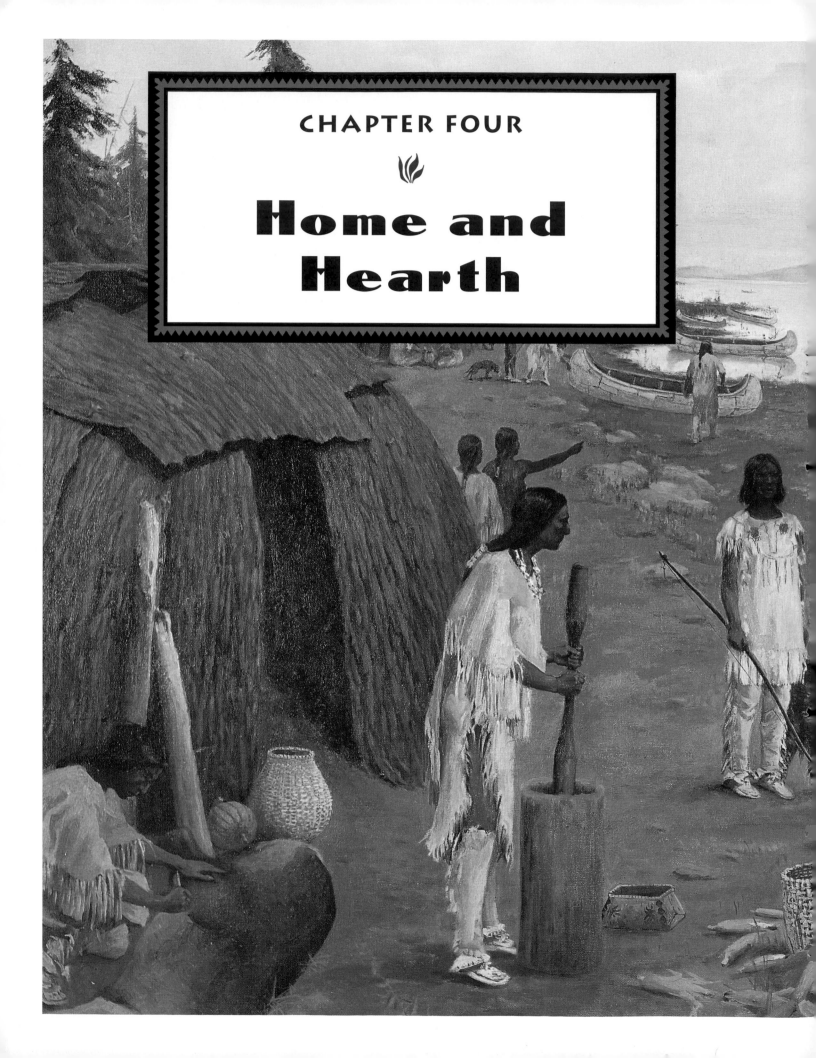

CHAPTER FOUR

Home and Hearth

❧ Childhood

From birth until the time a child learned to walk, he or she spent most of the time in a cradleboard. The cradleboard was made by attaching a footrest to the bottom of a wooden plank and a strip of bent wood to the top (to protect the baby's head should the cradleboard fall). The cradleboard was cushioned with moss or feathers, and then the baby was strapped on with leather strips or laced into a bed of soft animal skin attached to the cradleboard.

Parents often spent a great deal of time and care in making and decorating these cradleboards, which were often beautifully carved and adorned with shells, porcupine quill embroidery, and charms to protect the baby from sickness and evil. Safe in the cradleboard, the baby could sleep, watch what was going on (if the cradleboard was leaned upright or hung from a tree branch), or ride on the mother's back as she walked, the cradleboard hanging behind her from a band attached to her forehead.

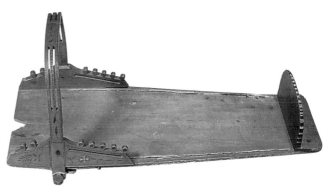

❧ **LEFT:** THIS SCENE SHOWS WHAT A TYPICAL DAY MIGHT HAVE BEEN LIKE IN AN ALGONQUIAN VILLAGE. BOTH MEN AND WOMEN WORKED AS THEIR CHILDREN HELPED THEM OR PLAYED NEARBY. **ABOVE:** A NORTHEAST WOODLANDS CRADLEBOARD

GREAT TURTLE ISLAND: A SENECA STORY

The Iroquois have several different versions of how the earth as we know it came to be. One version tells how a beautiful girl fell from the sky surrounded by a glow of light.

At this time, all people lived in a land in the sky because below, on Earth, there was no dry ground to support them. Earth was covered with water, and the only creatures that lived there were water animals like Otter, Muskrat, Loon, and Beaver. One day, in the land in the sky, a girl slipped through a hole made by an uprooted tree. The animals living in the water looked up and, seeing the glowing white light that surrounded the girl's body as she fell, they knew that she was a sacred being. They could not let her drown, so some of the animals dove down into the water, hoping to find some mud at the water's bottom for the girl to land upon. But the water was deep, and each animal that went below drowned before it could resurface with the mud. Finally, Muskrat went down and, after a long, long time, came back up, nearly drowned. In his paw was some mud, which the animals quickly placed on the back of Turtle. As soon as the mud was placed there, Turtle's shell began to grow. It grew so big that the girl was able to land safely. It eventually grew so big that it became the continent of North America, or, as the Iroquois call it, Great Turtle Island.

🔥 ANCIENT TRADITIONS AND LEGENDS CONTINUE TO INFLUENCE THE WORK OF MANY NATIVE AMERICAN ARTISTS TODAY. THIS CONTEMPORARY SCULPTURE WAS INSPIRED BY THE SENECA CREATION STORY OF GREAT TURTLE ISLAND.

Child rearing was mainly the responsibility of women. As she grew up, a female child would help take care of her younger brothers and sisters. Besides the help it offered her mother, this duty also prepared the girl to take care of her own children when she grew up and married.

Girls helped their mothers and adult female relatives with other tasks that they would someday take on fully as adult women. Women, who were associated with growth and fertility, did the farming, so a girl went to the fields with her mother to help with the planting and tending of the crops and out to gather wild berries and plants. At home, a girl helped to preserve these fruits and vegetables by drying them in the sun, and she helped to dry or smoke the meat and fish brought home by the men. She and her mother used any food that was not put away for later to cook delicious meals for the family.

Girls also learned from their female relatives how to soften hides (a process called "tanning"), how to sew, and how to make the family's clothing. Clothing in the Northeast consisted

WHEN GLASS BEADS BECAME AVAILABLE THROUGH TRADE WITH EUROPEANS, NATIVE AMERICAN WOMEN USED THESE BEAUTIFUL NEW DECORATIONS TO ADORN CLOTHING WITH ELABORATE FLORAL DESIGNS, AS SEEN ON THIS PAIR OF DYED BUCKSKIN MOCCASINS.

TRADING TEETH: A MOHAWK STORY

This is a tale some Woodland parents told their children to explain why young boys and girls lose their baby teeth:

Long ago, parents decided they would prefer the teeth of the beaver for their own children. As everyone knew, the beaver's teeth were more powerful than those of any other animal. At first the beaver agreed, but he later thought better of the bargain. How would he chop down trees with the small teeth of human children?

Even though the beaver had changed his mind, deciding to keep his own strong teeth, parents continued to throw their children's baby teeth as far as they could in the hopes that the beaver would again want to trade. This custom lasted for many years, until parents one day recognized that the Creator had indeed given each animal the teeth that were best suited to its own needs.

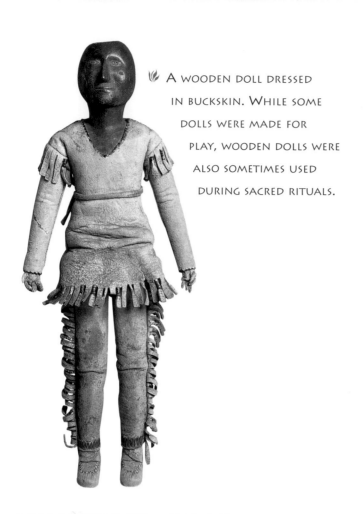

A WOODEN DOLL DRESSED IN BUCKSKIN. WHILE SOME DOLLS WERE MADE FOR PLAY, WOODEN DOLLS WERE ALSO SOMETIMES USED DURING SACRED RITUALS.

generally of breechclouts (loincloths), leggings, and shirts for men, and skirts, leggings, and shirts for women. Both men and women wore moccasins sewn from moose or deer hide.

Boys in the Northeast learned from their fathers and older male relatives the skills they would need as adults to care for their own families. Boys learned the importance of bravery in protecting their families and villages. They helped their fathers clear the fields for the women's planting. They learned how to make weapons and tools, how to fish, and how to be skillful hunters by going along on hunting trips when they were old enough.

When they were not helping with chores, boys and girls had plenty of free time for play. Toys were made from the materials at hand: girls played with dolls made of cornhusk or cattail while boys amused themselves with tops and toy bows and arrows. In addition to playing with toys, all children participated in games.

NAMING

Children were very precious to the Woodland peoples, and special care was taken in naming them. In some Woodland cultures the highest-ranking woman named each child in the community, but in other groups there were professional namers who had great skill in choosing a name that would suit the child. When the child reached adolescence, he or she might receive a new name, communicated by a spirit during a vision quest, a time of solitary prayer and fasting.

✹ Games and Amusements

Adults as well as children in the Northeast Woodlands enjoyed games and sports. Although some of these games were played as part of ceremonies, often they were played simply for fun. Ball games (balls were made of stuffed leather or wood), running races, and wrestling were all popular sports, as was the winter game of snowsnake, which was especially popular among the Iroquois. The snowsnake was a long, slender, wooden pole, specially carved so that it would travel swiftly. A player slid the snowsnake along a stretch of ice or frozen snow, and the person able to make it glide farthest was the winner.

LACROSSE: A WOODLANDS ORIGINAL

The game of lacrosse, enjoyed worldwide today, originated in the Woodlands of North America. Long before Europeans came to the New World, the ancient game was popular among Woodland peoples. The game was later given the name "lacrosse" by French settlers who thought the racketlike stick, which was made of bent wood, looked like a bishop's staff, called a "crosier."

Using their sticks, early Woodland players scored points by throwing the ball, which was made of either stuffed hide or wood, across the goal line of the opposing team. The ball could not be touched with the hands; it had to be thrown, carried, or caught using only the stick. Team members usually came from different villages and a game could last all day. Teams consisted of as few as ten players or as many as several hundred, and playing fields ranged in length from about one hundred to five hundred yards (91½ to 457m).

A rough and often violent game that required a great deal of speed, strength, and skill, lacrosse was often played as a type of warfare training. Today, lacrosse is still a popular sport in the Woodlands and around the world. In fact, the modern-day Iroquois have their own team, called the Iroquois Nationals, that competes worldwide.

EARLY LACROSSE STICKS

Games of chance, such as dice, were also popular. Dice were usually made by carving designs on sticks or painting designs on fruit pits. These were then thrown, and scoring depended on which designs landed face up. Other games, like ring and pin, tested a player's skill with hand-eye coordination. A "ring" could be a ball of corn-husk, the skull of a bird or rodent, or a piece of leather with holes punched in it. The "pin," a sharpened stick or piece of bone, was attached to the ring by a string or sinew and the player tried to catch the ring on the pin.

Games and sports provided energetic entertainment, but during quieter times, especially in winter when families were gathered around the warmth of the fires in the longhouses and wigwams, storytelling was a pastime enjoyed by all. Some stories were funny, and told about the adventures of tricksters and mischievous spirits. Others were more serious, and explained the origins of the people, the animals, and the earth. Stories explained how certain rituals and ceremonies were brought to the people and why they should be practiced. All stories, whether funny or serious, were lessons that taught children about the importance of leading a good life, about having respect for others, and about the values upheld by the community.

In addition to the entertainment provided by story-telling and games, peoples of the Northeast enjoyed social dancing to the sound of singing, rattles, and drums. Visiting each other's homes was another relaxing pastime that helped build a strong and stable community. Harvest time was a particularly good time for women to socialize. After the crops had been picked, women usually gathered together to remove the outer covering of the corn ears. These husking bees were also a source of recreation as people played games and entertained themselves with social dances.

❧ RACING CANOES WAS A POPULAR SPORT IN THE NORTHEAST WOODLANDS.

CHAPTER FIVE

Community Life

❦ Clans and Leaders

Each tribe, or nation, in the Northeast Woodlands consisted of extended families, or clans. Some clans were matrilineal (tracing descent through women), while others were patrilineal (tracing descent through men). The Iroquois, for example, were a matrilineal society. A woman's children, both male and female, belonged to her clan. When the woman's daughters had children, they would also belong to her clan. But her son's children would not belong to her clan; they would belong to the clan of their mother, and so on.

❦ **LEFT:** THIS DIORAMA DEPICTS AGRICULTURAL WOODLANDS INDIANS AT WORK. WHILE THE WOMEN HARVEST CORN, SQUASH, AND POTATOES, THE MEN GATHER AND CUT WOOD. **ABOVE:** THIS TRADITIONAL IROQUOIS HEADDRESS IS MADE OF FEATHERS AND ANIMAL SKIN. THE METAL BAND BECAME A COMMON FEATURE OF SUCH HEADDRESSES AFTER METALWORKING WAS INTRODUCED BY EUROPEANS.

WAMPUM: LITTLE BEADS OF SHELL

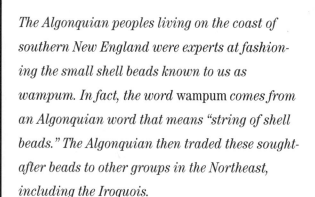

🌿 AN IROQUOIS WAMPUM BELT

The Algonquian peoples living on the coast of southern New England were experts at fashioning the small shell beads known to us as wampum. In fact, the word wampum comes from an Algonquian word that means "string of shell beads." The Algonquian then traded these sought-after beads to other groups in the Northeast, including the Iroquois.

Wampum beads were handcrafted one at a time, from whelk shells (to make white wampum) and quahog, or clam, shells (to make purple wampum). Traditionally, the beads were made by first trimming the shell with a stone hammer until it was down to a workable size. Then, using a sharp stone drill attached to a slender handle, one person rotated the drill's handle back and forth between his palms while another person held the shell. In this way a hole was made.

The shell was then polished with sand and strung on twine made from twisted plant fiber or sinews (animal tendons). In later times, after European contact, wampum was mass-produced by the Dutch using European tools. They sold wampum to European traders who traded it to the Woodland peoples, mainly for pelts. At one point, wampum was even used as a form of currency by European settlers when they had begun to run out of coins.

Strung as single or multiple strands, or woven into belts, wampum was used in a variety of ways by Northeast peoples. Wampum was used to decorate clothing and was worn as necklaces. It accompanied invitations, was given to mourners as a token of comfort, was given away at ceremonies, and was given or exchanged as a gift to commemorate a special event. For example, whenever individuals or groups reached an agreement regarding an important decision, wampum was exchanged. The designs on wampum strings or belts often served as reminders of important events. On certain occasions, wampum was "read" publicly as part of official meetings and ceremonies.

When an Iroquois woman married, her husband moved into the longhouse that she shared with other members of her clan. Clan names were often the names of animals. The Lenape, for example, had three clans: the Turkey, Turtle, and Wolf. The Iroquois had nine: the Bear, Deer, Snipe, Beaver, Wolf, Heron, Turtle, Eagle, and Eel. A person remained a member of his or her clan for life and could not marry a member of the same clan.

Among the Iroquois, women had a great deal of influence in choosing the tribal leaders. Tribal leaders, or chiefs, were elected by the clan heads, who were all women. Because men were often away for long periods of time hunting, trading, and making war, it made good sense to give women power over their clans. The clan

🌾 **ABOVE:** A YOUNG BOY WATCHES A WAMPUM MAKER DRILL A HOLE INTO A CLAM SHELL. WAMPUM WAS NEVER VIEWED AS MONEY BY THE WOODLAND PEOPLES, BUT WAS HIGHLY VALUED FOR GIFT-GIVING. **BELOW:** STRINGS OF WAMPUM

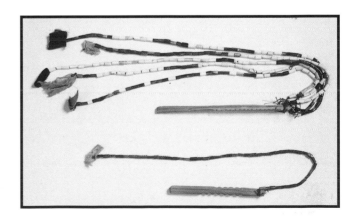

THE LEAGUE OF THE IROQUOIS

Iroquois tradition tells of an important event that united the Iroquois as the Five Nations. Accounts vary as to when this took place; some say it happened in the fifteenth century, while others say the sixteenth century.

Iroquois tradition explains how, before this union, the Senecas, Cayugas, Onondagas, Oneidas,

and Mohawks had been at war with one another. One man in particular was horrified by this situation, a holy man named Dekanawidah. Helped by a great orator (speaker) named Hiawatha, Dekanawidah began to spread the message that the Iroquois nations should come together and live in harmony with one another. Eventually, the five nations agreed and this political alliance became known as the League of the Iroquois, or the Iroquois Confederacy.

This map shows the location of the original Five Nations of the Iroquois Confederacy. Placed beside one another, the Five Nations resembled a traditional longhouse, and sometimes they even referred to their confederacy as "the longhouse."

LAKE ONTARIO

COUNCIL FIRE
X

WESTERN DOOR

SENECA
CAYUGA
ONONDAGA
ONEIDA
MOHAWK

EASTERN DOOR

LAKE ERIE

MAP OF
NEW YORK
SHOWING
PLAN OF
THE LONG HOUSE
OF THE FIVE NATIONS

heads chose leaders according to their abilities; they had to be wise decision-makers and set a good example for the community. Because women raised the children, they were best suited to decide who would make good leaders. Chiefs did not rule the community; rather, decisions were made by councils of adult members of the community under the chief's leadership. In council, issues were discussed and the chiefs offered advice based on their experience and wisdom. Before a decision was made to take action, the decision had to be agreed upon by all members of the community. A chief kept his

position for life, but if he was not doing a good job, he could be removed from his position by the same clan heads who had appointed him.

Although systems of government varied throughout the Northeast, leaders generally were, as among the Iroquois, respected members of the community who counciled rather than ruled. A leader had many responsibilities, including keeping peace within the community, helping to organize the various community ceremonies and celebrations, and meeting with visitors from other villages.

🌿 Spiritual Life

At the heart of the spiritual traditions of the Northeast peoples was the idea that humans were only a part of the natural world around them. The plants and animals of the forests, the fish and water of the streams, and the rocks and trees of the mountains were all alive with their own life forces, just like humans. When taking from the environment, whether it was an animal hunted or a plant picked, it was necessary to give something back in the form of a prayer or an offering of tobacco.

Northeast peoples had a great variety of rituals and ceremonies that showed respect for the natural world and gave thanks to the spirits that dwelled around them. Almost all groups that farmed had some form of the Green Corn Ceremony. This community celebration offered thanks to the earth for bringing forth this important crop and showed appreciation for the corn itself, which offered nourishment. Among the Iroquois, ceremonies were held throughout the year in gratitude for various foods. For example, the Strawberry Ceremony, held in spring, gave thanks for the newly ripening strawberries; the

🌿 **RIGHT:** "CORN SPIRIT," A SCULPTURE BY THE CONTEMPORARY ARTIST STAN HILL, REFLECTS THE IMPORTANCE OF CORN TO THE ORIGINAL PEOPLES OF THE NORTHEAST.
BELOW: TOBACCO, USED BY NATIVE AMERICANS FOR SMOKING AND AS OFFERINGS TO THE SPIRITS, IS A CROP THAT IS NATIVE TO THE WESTERN HEMISPHERE.

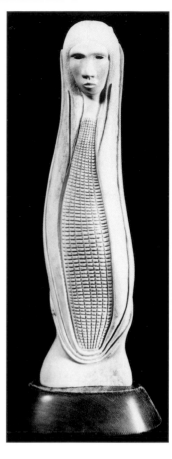

THE IROQUOIS CALENDAR

The Iroquois marked the passing of the year with festivals that celebrated their link with nature. Most festivals followed the same pattern and often lasted several days. Speakers gave thanks to the spirits for the bounty of the earth. Ceremonial dances and great feasts were also part of the celebrations. Sometimes, men of the village sang their own songs to the spirits. Games of chance, such as the bowl game, were often played as part of the rituals. In the bowl game six peach pits that had been colored white on one side and black on the other were placed in a wooden bowl. The player hit the bowl on the ground, and if five or six of the peach pits turned up with the same color, the player got another turn. Otherwise, play passed to the opposing team.

This list shows the main festivals and when they occurred.

Midwinter Ceremony *(late January or early February)*
Celebrated the Iroquois New Year and served as a time of renewal of dreams.

Rise of the Maple Ceremony *(late February or March, depending on sap levels)*
Gave thanks for the sap that would sweeten many dishes.

Planting of Corn Ceremony *(May or June)*
Blessed the seeds in order to assure a bountiful harvest.

Strawberry Ceremony *(June)*
Showed gratitude for the first fruit.

Green Corn Ceremony *(July or August)*
Honored the all-important corn plant.

Harvest Ceremony *(October)*
Celebrated a successful reaping of crops.

autumn Harvest Ceremony gave thanks to all crops; and the Midwinter Ceremony, held in January, gave thanks to the Creator and all things.

While some ceremonies involved the whole community, some were more intimate and personal. When young men and women reached adolescence, for example, they often went out alone to a secluded spot in the forest to fast and pray in the hope of receiving a visit from a guardian spirit. Spiritual journeys such as these could be taken throughout a person's life to strengthen the person's ties to the spiritual world.

Some rituals in the Northeast honored the dead and showed respect for the spirits of the ancestors. A ceremony known as the Feast of the Dead was held by the

Huron about every ten to twelve years. During the Feast of the Dead, those individuals who had died in the years since the last Feast of the Dead were taken from the cemetery and brought to the village. There they were honored with feasting and dancing before being re-buried. This ceremony was held to please the spirits of the departed relatives and to send them off happily to the world of the dead.

Still other rituals and ceremonies in the Northeast were held to heal the sick and suffering. All Northeast groups had individuals who were well known for their abilities to heal. During special ceremonies, medicine men and women called on the spirit world for help in healing a patient. These people were also skilled in using herbal remedies, which were given to the patient as part of the ceremony.

Many Northeast groups had medicine societies made up of a number of healers. One such medicine society of the Great Lakes peoples was the Midewiwin, a secret organization whose rituals were considered to be very powerful and effective in curing people. Members of the Midewiwin kept otter-skin medicine bags containing the items used in rituals. They recorded the rituals, including the stories, songs, and remedies associated with them, by incising symbols, called "pictographs," on birch-bark scrolls using a "pen" of sharpened bone.

RIGHT: AN OTTER-SKIN MEDICINE BAG OF THE MIDEWIWIN SOCIETY, USED TO HOLD THE RITUAL ITEMS OF SOCIETY MEMBERS. SUCH BAGS WERE USU-ALLY DECORATED WITH FLORAL DESIGNS MADE WITH PORCUPINE QUILLS OR, IN LATER TIMES, GLASS BEADS, RIBBON, AND COTTON CLOTH. **BELOW:** BIRCH-BARK PLAQUES WERE OFTEN DECORATED BY ETCHING DESIGNS INTO THE BARK WITH A SHARP TOOL.

CONCLUSION

❧

Modern Woodland Life

Beginning in the sixteenth century, European explorers and commercial fishermen began traveling to the Northeast Woodlands. These fishermen began by first establishing camps along the coast of Newfoundland to cure their fish. Toward the end of the century, they began to move south along the coast of New England.

During the same century the Northeast saw the beginnings of the fur trade, which rapidly expanded through the seventeenth century. Europeans, realizing that the abundance of fur-bearing animals in the area offered a profitable business, began a trade relationship with Native American trappers. The trappers exchanged furs such as beaver, marten, and fox for European goods such as iron knives and axes, glass beads, cloth, and guns. This relationship lasted well into the nineteenth century.

As the fur trade expanded, hostilities arose among neighboring groups in the Northeast as each tried to maintain control of the trade. Contact with European traders brought about another problem: European diseases. Epidemics of diseases such as smallpox, measles, and scarlet fever killed large numbers of Native Americans. Estimates vary, but reports state that many groups lost as much as half their population.

During the seventeenth century, colonists also began to arrive from England, France, and Holland, setting up permanent settlements in various areas along the Atlantic coast. The first of these colonies was Jamestown, established by English colonists in Virginia in 1607. With the arrival of Europeans came Christianity, and many people of the Northeastern groups were converted to this newly introduced religion. In the following century, some groups in the

Northeast became involved in the war between the French and English, who were each fighting to gain control over North America.

With all the changes brought about by contact with Europeans over the past five hundred years, peoples of the Northeast Woodlands have managed to suc-

🌿 CONTACT WITH EUROPEANS BROUGHT ABOUT MANY CHANGES FOR PEOPLES OF THE NORTHEAST. ONE SUCH CHANGE WAS THE INTRODUCTION OF NEW ITEMS THROUGH TRADE. THIS NINETEENTH-CENTURY PAINTING SHOWS A GROUP OF CHIPPEWA PLAYING THE EUROPEAN GAME OF CHECKERS.

cessfully retain many of their customs and traditions. Many rituals and ceremonies are still practiced today and remain an important part of the spiritual life of Woodland peoples. Artisans still create beautiful items out of birch bark, cornhusks, and carved wood. Many modern Native American artists, writers, and musicians of the Northeast create art, stories, and songs based on the ideas and teachings of their people.

🌿 A MODERN SENECA FAMILY. TODAY, MANY NORTHEAST PEOPLES CONTINUE TO WEAR THE TRADITIONAL DRESS OF THEIR ANCESTORS FOR SPECIAL CEREMONIES AND CELEBRATIONS.

Rooted in ancient beliefs and practices, tradition still plays an important role for the Native Americans of the Northeast Woodlands.

🔥 World Time Line

6000 B.C.–1000 B.C.

The Northeast:

The Northeast is in the Archaic period (about 6000 B.C.–1500 B.C.), during which the people hunt and gather food and make stone tools; two cultures, the Old Copper Culture (about 3000 B.C.–1000 B.C.) and the Red Paint People (about 2000 B.C. to 500 B.C.), develop.

The World:

The Neolithic Age, which is characterized by the use of polished stone implements, occurs in Europe (about 4000 B.C.–2400 B.C.); the Sumerians develop cuneiform writing (about 3000 B.C.); Egypt's largest pyramid is built at Giza (about 2500 B.C.); King Hammurabi rules the Babylonian Empire (1792 B.C.–1750 B.C.); the Bronze Age begins in China (about 1600 B.C.).

1000 B.C.–A.D. 1600

The Northeast:

The Northeast is in the Woodland Period (about 1000 B.C. to the sixteenth century), during which the people developed agriculture, began making pottery, and devoted much attention to the ritual burying of the dead in domed mounds of earth; the Adena (about 1000 B.C.–A.D. 200) and the Hopewell (about 200 B.C.–A.D. 500) traditions develop; European explorers and commercial fishermen begin to arrive (early 1500s).

The World:

Hinduism develops in India (probably about 1000 B.C.); the Roman city of Pompeii is destroyed (A.D. 79); Maya civilization flourishes in Mexico (about A.D. 500); a "Golden Age" flourishes in China under the Tang Dynasty (A.D. 618–907); the Islamic Empire is at its peak (about A.D. 850); Marco Polo sets out to explore Asia (1271); the University at Timbuktu in Africa is established (about A.D. 1450); the Renaissance is under way in Europe (A.D. 1300s–1500s).

✺ Glossary

Adena
A culture that arose in the Ohio Valley about 1000 B.C., when people began to bury their dead in artificial mounds of earth.

annealing
The process of strengthening copper by heating it and then plunging it into cold water over and over again.

Archaic Period
The archaeological period that lasted in the Northeast Woodlands from about 6000 B.C. to about 1500 B.C.

clan
An extended family. In a matrilineal society, clan members belong to the clan of their mothers. In a patrilineal society, clan members belong to the clan of their fathers.

cradleboard
A cradle (made of wood in the Northeast) used to carry babies.

earthwork
Ridges of piled earth made into some form, like the geometric shapes made by the peoples of the Adena and Hopewell traditions.

effigy
A symbolic figure, usually of an animal or person.

grave goods
Items buried with individuals.

Great Serpent Mound
An impressive earthwork in Ohio, shaped like a snake with an egg in its mouth.

Hopewell
A tradition that arose in the Ohio Valley about 200 B.C. Hopewell peoples, relying on a vast trade network of exotic materials, buried their dead in earthen mounds filled with elaborate grave goods.

kame
A small hill made by the movement of glaciers.

Koster
An important Northeast Woodland archaeological site, located in present-day Illinois.

lacrosse
The Eastern Woodland sport of stickball, so named by French settlers.

longhouse
A large Northeast Woodland home with a barrel-shaped roof that housed several related families.

matrilineal	Tracing descent through the mother's bloodline.	**Paleo-Indians**	The term given to the Native Americans living during the last Ice Age.
Meadowcroft Rockshelter	An important Northeast Woodland archaeological site located in present-day Pennsylvania.	**patrilineal**	Tracing descent through the father's bloodline.
Midewiwin	A secret and powerful organization of the Great Lakes peoples made up of traditional healers.	**Red Paint People**	A culture that developed about 2000 B.C., so named because of the people's custom of lining burial pits with the mineral red hematite.
Mississippian	An early tradition arising in the Mississippi Valley that was widespread in the Southeast Woodlands but reached into the Midwest.	**succotash**	A Woodland dish made with corn, beans, and squash.
Mound Builders	The name given to the peoples of the Adena and Hopewell traditions because of their practice of burying their dead in earthen mounds.	**wampum**	Shell beads strung into strands or belts and used ceremonially by Northeast peoples.
		wigwam	A Northeast Woodland home, often dome-shaped, used mainly by Algonquian peoples.
Old Copper Culture	A culture that developed in the western Great Lakes area about 3000 B.C. whose people mined and fashioned copper.	**Woodland Period**	The archaeological period that lasted in the Northeast from about 1000 B.C. to the point of European contact.

Resources

Books

Concise Encyclopedia of the American Indian.
  Bruce Grant (Random House)

The Encyclopedia of Native America. Trudy
  Griffin-Pierce (Viking)

*Exploring Ancient Native America: An Archaeological
  Guide.* David Hurst Thomas (Macmillan)

Handbook of Northeastern Indian Medicinal Plants.
  James A. Duke (Quarterman Publications)

The Indian Heritage of America. Alvin M. Joseph, Jr.
  (Portland House)

Indian Tribes of North America. Joseph Sherman
  (Portland House)

Indians of the Northeast. Colin G. Calloway
  (Facts on File)

*Native Americans of the Northeast. Indians of North
  America Set.* (Chelsea House)

*Return of the Sun: Native American Tales from
  the Northeast Woodlands.* Joseph Bruchac
  (Crossing Press)

*The Smithsonian Book of North American Indians:
  Before the Coming of the Europeans.*
  (Smithsonian Books)

*Trading Identities: The Souvenir in Native American
  Art from the Northeast, 1700-1900.* Ruth B. Phillips
  (University of Washington Press)

*When the Chenoo Howls: Native American Tales
  of Terror.* Joseph and James Bruchac
  (Walker and Company)

Videos

*America's Great Indian Nations: Iroquois, Seminoles,
  Navajo, Cheyenne, Lakota.* (Questar Video)

*Dancing in Moccasins: Keeping Native American
  Traditions Alive.* (Films for the Humanities and
  Sciences)

Discovering American Indian Music. (Encyclopedia
  Britannica Educational Corporation)

How to Trace Your Native American Heritage. (Jeffrey
  Norton Publishers, Inc.)

The Native Americans. The Nations of the Northeast.
  (Turner Home Entertainment)

Pow wow. (Schlessinger Video Productions)

Web Sites

National Museum of the American Indian
www.si.edu/nmai/

Native Web
www.nativeweb.org/

Oneida Indian Nation
www.oneida-nation.net/

Potawatomi Indians
www.danville.net/~grf/

Northeast Woodlands Pottery
www.nativetech.org/pottery/pottery.htm

Pocahontas
www.apva.org/history/pocahont.html

Photo-graphy Credits

Front jacket photograph: ©Art Resource, NY/Werner Forman Archive

American Museum of Natural History/Courtesy Department Library Services: Neg. #326059: p.15; A.A. Jansson/Neg. #1582: pp. 40-41; Julius Kirschner/Neg. #15117: p. 36 right, Neg. #315467: pp. 48-49; C. Knight/Neg. #2432: pp. 16-17; Kay C. Lenskjold/Neg. #38575: p. 33; H.S. Rice/Neg. #280003: p. 38 bottom

Archive Photos: p. 34

Art Resource: National Museum of American Art, Smithsonian Institution, Washington D.C.: pp. 2, 46-47; Werner Forman Archive: pp. 18, 20, 23, 25, 26 both

©Alan Detrick: p. 13 top left

Envision: ©Ronald Partis: p. 35 top; ©Sue Pashko: p. 35 bottom

FPG International: p. 57; ©Jim Mejuto: p. 58; ©Maria Pape: p. 39 top

Iroquois Indian Museum, Howes Cave, NY: pp. 42, 53 top

Leo de Wys: ©Henryk Kaiser: pp. 8-9

Courtesy National Park Service: p. 17; ©Eastern National: painting by Louis S. Glanzman: pp. 24-25

Courtesy of The National Museum of the American Indian/ Smithsonian Institution: Neg. # 1548: p. 25; Neg. #3129: p. 27 bottom; Neg.#1874: p. 39 bottom; Neg. #3498: p. 41; Neg. #1558: pp. 5 right, 43; Neg. #3468: p. 49; Neg. #29163: p. 50; Neg. #38194: p. 51 bottom; Neg. #28406: p. 52; Neg. #3886: p. 55 left

Emilya Naymark: All map illustrations

North Wind Picture Archive: pp. 9, 11, 12 bottom right, 14, 22, 29, 38 top

Ohio Historical Society: p. 21

Peabody Museum: ©Hillel Burger: p. 45

Royal Ontario Museum: pp. 30-31

Superstock: pp. 37; 51 top

Thaw Collection/Fenimore House Museum, Cooperstown, NY: ©John Bigelow Taylor: pp. 5, 27 top, 31, 44, 55 right

Tony Stone Images: p. 36 left; ©Tom Raymond: p. 53 bottom ©Jon Riley: p. 7

The Wildlife Collection: ©Kenneth A. Deitcher: p. 13 middle right; ©Michael Francis: pp. 12 top left, 32; ©D. Robert Franz: p. 12 bottom left; ©Henry Holdsworth: p. 12 middle right; ©Ralph Lee Hopkins: p. 13 bottom right; ©Chris Huss: p. 13 middle left; ©Robert Lankinen: p. 12 top right; ©Clay Myers: p.13 top middle and bottom left; ©Gary Schultz: p. 13 top right; ©Tom Vezo: p. 12 middle left

Index